Marie Curie

Ann Fullick

Heinemann Library
Chicago, Illinois

Designed by AMR
Originated by Ambassador Litho
Printed in Hong Kong

05 04 03 02 01
10 9 8 7 6 5 4 3 2 1

Library of Congress Cataloging-in-Publication Data
Fullick, Ann, 1956-
    Marie Curie / Ann Fullick.
      p. cm. – (Groundbreakers)
    Includes bibliographical references and index.
    Summary: A biography of the chemist whose work with radium laid the foundation for
much of today's scientific knowledge.
    ISBN 1-57572-374-3 (library)
    1. Curie, Marie, 1867-1934—Juvenile literature. 2.
Chemists—Poland—Biography—Juvenile literature. 3. Women
scientists—Biography—Juvenile literature. [1. Curie, Marie, 1867-1934. 2. Chemists. 3.
Women—Biography.] I. Title. II. Series.

QD22.C8 F85 2000
540'.92—dc21
[B]   00-024352

Acknowledgments
The Publishers would like to thank the following for permission to reproduce photographs:
Mary Evans Picture Library, pp. 4, 5, 9, 13, 14, 20, 27, 28; Robert Harding Picture Library,
pp. 17, 39; Hulton Getty, pp. 18, 19, 23; Science Photo Library/C. Powell, P. Fowler, D. Perkins,
p. 26; Science Photo Library/J. C. Revy, p. 24; Science Photo Library/Jean-Loup Charmet, p. 25;
Corbis, pp. 31, 34; Science Photo Library/James Stevenson, p. 32; Hulton Deutsch, p. 37;
Science Photo Library/Peter Menzel, p. 38; Popperfoto, pp. 40, 41.

Cover photograph reproduced with permission of Sipa Press.

Every effort has been made to contact copyright holders of any material reproduced in this
book. Any omissions will be rectified in subsequent printings if notice is given to the publisher.

Some words are shown in bold, **like this.** You can find out what
they mean by looking in the glossary.

Contents

The Polish Homeland

On November 7, 1867, a Polish teacher gave birth to the last of her five children, a daughter named Marya. Madame Sklodovska had no idea what kind of future lay ahead for the little girl—who would always be known as "Manya" by her family, but as Marie Curie by the rest of the world. In the late nineteenth century, Poland was not an easy place to live. A century before, Poland had been weak, and her greedy neighbors—Prussia (now part of Germany), Russia, and Austria—had **annexed** the country and divided it between them. The Poles had on several occasions tried to overthrow their new rulers, so now people such as Manya's family, who lived in Russian Poland, had a very tough existence. They were threatened with execution or **banishment** to Siberia if they rebelled.

Life under Russian rule

A stream of policemen, professors, and minor **dignitaries** was sent from Russia to oversee the whole of Polish life. They watched over the people and looked for signs of rebellion—such as criticizing Russia, or speaking Polish instead of Russian.

Polish intellectuals and teachers, like Marie Curie's father, were not allowed to think freely, and they even had to teach in Russian rather than Polish. The Catholic religion of the Poles was frowned upon, and children had to learn Russian history and Russian folk stories in school.

This is a busy market in nineteenth-century Warsaw. Polish landowners and farmers were kept poor under Russian rule.

Marie Curie, shown here in 1911, used the amazing power and focus of her mind in dedicating her whole life to science.

The scientific view of the world

At the time of Marie Curie's birth, many dedicated people were making significant advances in scientific discovery, changing the way people thought about the world. Charles Darwin had published his great book on evolution, *The Origin of Species,* in 1859. Faraday, Maxwell, and Boltzmann had advanced the understanding of the links between magnetism and electricity. And in chemistry, Dmitri Mendeleev had published his **periodic table,** the basis of the one we still use now. However, many of the **elements** we know today were still undiscovered—and this is where Marie Curie stepped in.

In a lifetime's work of sheer brilliance, Marie would discover not one, but two, new elements. She would make great advances in the understanding of **radioactivity** and develop new treatments for **cancer** that are still being used today.

Enter Marya Sklodovska

The girl who would be known as Marie Curie was born to loving, lively-minded parents. Vladislav Sklodovski was the son of an important Polish family who, like so many others in 19th-century Poland, had fallen on hard times. He was an intellectual who taught mathematics and **physics** in Warsaw, the capital of Poland. His wife, a woman of great beauty and intelligence, was also a teacher and the principal of a private girls' school in Warsaw, until shortly after Marya was born. In Poland, men's names end with "i" and women's with "a," so Marya's father's name was Sklodovski and her mother's was Sklodovska.

The couple had five children: four girls and a boy. In their early years, the Sklodovski children had a comfortable home, exciting holidays in the countryside with relatives, and lots of love and attention from their devoted parents.

Early promise...

Marya became a fluent reader at only four years old. She was very interested in her father's scientific instruments—the barometer, the tubes, the scales, and the gold leaf electroscope. As a child, she had an amazing memory, and could soon speak Russian as well as her native Polish. She shone in all her classes at school.

Marya (Marie, center) and her siblings—Zosia, Hela, Joseph, and Bronya (left to right)—were a close-knit unit who supported each other throughout their lives.

6

Marya's mother's early death left her children with a lasting sense of responsibility for their father.

...early shadows

Little Marya was very close to her mother, and loved to spend time with her. But after the birth of her last daughter, Madame Sklodovska developed **tuberculosis,** and the dreadful disease gradually took hold and spread. She never allowed herself to kiss and hug her children, in case she might infect them. Often, the older sisters looked after the youngest to relieve their exhausted mother.

In the autumn of 1873, Marie's father was publicly disgraced because he did not show enough respect to the Russian principal of the school in which he taught. He also lost most of his savings through bad business deals. The family moved to a smaller home and rented out rooms. One of their boarders infected Bronya and Zosia with **typhus** in 1874. Zosia, the oldest, could not overcome the fever and died. Little Marya was only nine when she went to her big sister's funeral.

Just two years later, her beloved mother lost her fight with tuberculosis. "I love you," she whispered to her husband and children on her deathbed. The shadow of grief fell heavily on the little family now remaining. Young Marya learned early that life can be very cruel.

7

The Teenage Years

Marya grew up rapidly, along with her brother and sisters. Her teenage years were a time for enjoying life and trying out new ideas before shouldering the burdens of responsibility and adulthood.

Bronya won a gold medal as the most outstanding student when she left school. So did Joseph, Marie's only brother. Both wanted to become doctors, but only Joseph went on to Warsaw University to study medicine. Bronya stayed at home to take care of the family, replacing the housekeepers who had run the house following their mother's death. Women were not allowed to study at Warsaw University, so Bronya applied herself to running a happy home for her father, brother, and sisters.

In Curie's words:

In this letter written by Marie Curie (age 13) to her friend Kazia Przyborovska, she confesses—a little embarrassed—that she loves school. The two girls were best friends who went everywhere together.

"Do you know, Kazia, in spite of everything I like school. Perhaps you will make fun of me, but nevertheless I must tell you that I like it, and even that I love it. I can realize that now."

The star student

Meanwhile, Marya made great progress at school. She loved the experience of learning, in spite of the problems involved in being taught in Russian. Classes were a mix of Russian, Polish, and German girls, many of whom, like her, were learning in a second language.

In June 1883, Marya Sklodovska left secondary school, promising to keep in touch with all her girlhood friends forever. She, too, was awarded the gold medal for best student.

A year in the country

However, the strain of Marya's hard work had worn her out. Her father decided that his youngest daughter should have a year's vacation in the countryside before deciding how she would earn her living. This is the only record we have of Marie Curie not working—just simply enjoying herself—for any length of time. She spent her time exploring, boating, swimming, reading novels, and going to dances and parties with her cousins and friends. At the St. Louis night ball, which she remembered clearly all her life, she wore out a new pair of shoes dancing the night away.

Trips to balls and parties in sleighs like this were part of the magic for Marya in her year off. As she wrote to her dear friend Kazia: "I can't believe geometry or algebra ever existed. I have completely forgotten them."

A Very Special Governess

After her year off, Marya returned to the real world quickly, giving lessons to wealthy children to earn some money. At the same time, she and her sister Bronya joined the "Floating University," a group that met illegally in secret places and provided instruction and discussion for those too poor to go to a university in Poland. The group also included many women, who were not accepted at Warsaw University. These young people then shared their knowledge with those even poorer than themselves.

Bronya's future

Marya's brother, Joseph, was doing well in his training to be a doctor. Hela was unsure whether to be a teacher or a singer, but was obviously going to do well at either—or both. Bronya, however, was stuck. She had run the household for years, but what she really wanted was to go to Paris and study medicine, then return to Poland to practice as a doctor. However, there was no money to make this dream come true. Marya, who was particularly close to Bronya, came up with a clever plan to make the impossible happen.

Marya's plan

At just eighteen years of age, Marya became a **governess** to support her older sister at medical school. She was highly intelligent and could speak Polish, German, Russian, and other languages, but she was determined that twenty-year-old Bronya should have her chance. When Bronya was finished, it would be Marya's turn.

To enable Bronya to become a doctor, Marya (left) put her own ambitions aside and resigned herself to becoming a governess.

Being a governess was not as easy as Marya had thought it would be. She hated her first job and left after a few weeks. Then she took another job far from her beloved home and family. However, although she was homesick, she enjoyed working with the children in her care. The family treated her well, and after a time, she began to teach the poor children of the local village to read, helped by Bronka, the oldest daughter in the family.

First love, first heartbreak

When Casimir, the oldest son of the family, came home from Warsaw University for the holidays, he fell in love with the new, talented, and attractive governess—and Marya fell in love with him. They planned to marry, but the family would not hear of it. Casimir gave in to their wishes, and Marya was heartbroken. She could not leave her job—too many people depended on her earnings—so for another two years she stayed, nursing her sadness in the home of these people who were happy to employ her as governess, but would not consider her as a daughter-in-law. Although she did not know it at the time, this was a blessing in disguise.

Marya worked as a governess for three long years at this house in Poland.

The Tide Turns

In her years as a **governess,** Marya gave up all hope of ever studying in Paris herself. Eventually, however, things began to move in her favor, though she found this hard to accept.

In 1888, Marya's father, Vladislav Sklodovski, retired. Instead of sitting and enjoying his retirement, though, he immediately took another job at a difficult school with a very good salary. This, combined with his **pension,** allowed him to begin to support his family again. Bronya began to pay Marya back, so she could build up some savings.

The first chance

Then in 1890, when Bronya was nearly qualified to be a doctor, she married Casimir Dluski, who was already a doctor. She wrote to her sister, asking her to come to Paris. Marya's chance had come—yet she turned it down. She felt that the family still needed her support and energy; besides, she was still in love with her own Casimir. She did not want to leave Poland for France and lose her chance of love.

Vladislav Sklodovski, Marya (left), Bronya, and Hela posed in 1890, just as the family fortunes were improving a little.

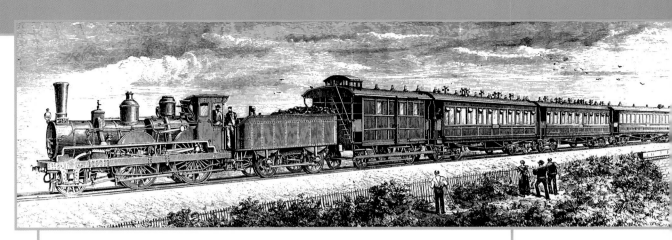

Marya sent almost everything she would need on to Paris ahead of her. Finally, she hugged her father and boarded a train like this one, which would take her to Paris, her studies, and her destiny.

A second chance

While Marya was in Warsaw, a very important opportunity came her way. She met up again with her friends in the "Floating University," and this time she got the opportunity to study in a secret laboratory. Disguised from the authorities during the day as a museum, the laboratory was really used to teach practical science to young Poles.

Struggling to carry out experiments which she had previously only read about, Marya was gripped with a great excitement. She now knew, quite certainly, what she wanted to study—she had to be a scientist.

In spite of his parents' disapproval, Casimir and Marya stayed in touch, although he would not make a commitment to her. In September 1891, they vacationed together in the mountains, where Marya finally realized this was not the man for her. Her true vocation lay in Paris, and with science. She could not wait to get home and write to Bronya, and she was soon on her way to Paris. Little did she guess what lay ahead of her—or that she would never live in Poland again.

In Curie's words:

"Now, Bronya…Decide if you can really take me in at your house, for I can come now. I have enough to pay all my expenses…You can put me up anywhere…I promise that I shall not be a bore or create disorder. I implore you to answer me…"

The Student

Within a few weeks of making her decision to go to Paris, Marie Sklodovska enrolled in the Faculty of Sciences at the Sorbonne, the famous Paris university—one of only 23 women to do so. She registered using the French version of her name—Marie, rather than Marya. This was how she was known from then on.

Once Marie was established as a student, she gave everything to her studies. She put very little effort into socializing, so many of her fellow students did not even know her name.

When Marie first arrived in Paris, she lived with Bronya and her husband, Casimir Dluski, in a small apartment an hour from the school. They both worked as doctors and led a busy social life. Much as Marie loved their company, she felt that it kept her from working, so she decided to rent a tiny attic of her own, close to the university. The fact that she had little money and did not know how to cook even simple meals did not stop her.

*At the Sorbonne, Marie quickly realized that there were some very large gaps in her knowledge, yet she was blissfully happy, spending her days absorbed in the study of mathematics, **physics**, and chemistry.*

In Curie's words:

During her hard student days, Marie wrote occasional pieces of poetry, which she kept all her life. These poems show that she actually embraced and enjoyed the hard path she had chosen:

"Ah! How harshly the youth of the student passes,
While all around her, with passions ever fresh,
Other youths search eagerly for easy pleasures!
And yet in solitude
She lives, obscure and blessed,
For in her cell she finds the ardor
That makes her heart immense."

But living in freezing conditions and hardly eating took its toll, and eventually, she collapsed. Bronya and Casimir spent a week feeding her well and making her rest—and then she returned to her attic to do the same thing again.

The gifted student

Marie was not content to earn just one **master's degree**—she worked for two: one in physics, and the other in mathematics. At the same time, she perfected her French until she could speak like a native. When the exam results were announced, all her efforts were rewarded—she was first in the class!

Marie went home to Poland for a summer vacation, returning healthy, rested, and plump from all the food she had been given while she was at home. However, she returned to work and neglected herself again. In 1893, money was tight, and Marie's studies were threatened until she won a Polish **scholarship,** ensuring that her academic career was safe for the next fifteen months. Full of excitement, she rushed back to Paris and her beloved laboratories.

Pierre Curie

Pierre Curie (in back, on the right) came from a close and supportive family, and he and his brother were both brilliant scientists.

In Curie's words:

Marie later reflected on her first impressions of Pierre:
"He seemed very young to me, although he was then aged thirty-five. I was struck by his clear gaze and by the slight appearance of carelessness in his lofty stature …his smile, at once grave and youthful, inspired confidence."

Marie was asked to carry out a study on the magnetic properties of various steels, but needed space to complete the work. She asked a visiting Polish professor, who invited her to tea with someone he thought might be able to help—a renowned young scientist named Pierre Curie.

The life of Pierre Curie

Pierre Curie was born in Paris on May 15, 1859. He had an older brother, Jacques, and his father and grandfather were both doctors. Pierre was a brilliant child, but he was dreamy and a bit of a loner. His father had a quick temper, but he was also a considerate and intelligent man. He realized that school would not suit Pierre, so he educated his son at home, allowing Pierre's mind to expand at its own rapid pace. Pierre's mother was cheerful and an expert housekeeper. The boys had a very happy childhood, full of intellectual stimulation and fun in the woods surrounding their home.

By the time Pierre was eighteen, he had a **master's degree** in physics—most students do not achieve a master's degree until their twenties. For a number of years, he and Jacques worked together, developing **piezoelectric quartz,** which allows tiny **voltages** to be measured with great precision. In 1883, the brothers reluctantly separated.

Jacques became a professor at Montpellier far away in southern France, and Pierre was chief of the laboratory at the School of Industrial Physics and Chemistry of the City of Paris. A few years later, Pierre Curie developed an ultrasensitive scientific scale that became known as the "Curie scale." He then discovered a fundamental law governing the relationship between temperature and magnetism, which is called "Curie's law."

Pierre the man

Pierre Curie was tall and graceful, with a full beard, and quite attractive with his dark, burning eyes. However, after a disastrous early love affair, he lost interest in romance—his whole focus as a young man was his work. Anything that distracted him from his physics was a nuisance, and, as he wrote in his diary, "Women of genius are rare...."

At 35, Pierre was a successful but impoverished scientist, who seemed destined to lead a solitary life dedicated to his work. His chance meeting with Marie Sklodovska would change all that for good.

The only distraction Pierre Curie allowed himself was a love of the countryside around Alsace, in northeastern France. Walking and biking were passions of his, which he enjoyed during his vacations.

Love and Marriage

At their first meeting, Pierre Curie and Marie Sklodovska found themselves drawn to each other. It was a meeting of two great minds, and they were soon deep in conversation about **physics.** From this simple beginning grew one of the greatest scientific partnerships the world has ever known.

Pierre Curie was amazed by his response to Marie—he could not stop thinking about her. After several meetings, he gave her a gift—a copy of his latest publication, "On Symmetry in Physical Phenomena: Symmetry of an Electric Field and of a Magnetic Field." He wrote on the first page: "To Mlle. (Mademoiselle or Miss) Sklodovska, with the respect and friendship of the author, P. Curie."

Pierre was eight years older than Marie, and he was the first to declare his love. It took Marie more than a year to make up her mind. Marrying Pierre, and working with him in Paris, meant giving up for good her idea of returning to Poland to live with her father and teach. Finally, however, she could deny her feelings no longer.

When Marie Sklodovska finally agreed to marry Pierre Curie, she committed herself to a life in Paris, and never lived in her native Poland again.

The wedding took place on July 26, 1895. Instead of being married in a church, Marie and Pierre had a simple civil ceremony, followed by a small gathering of their closest family and friends at the house of Pierre's parents in Sceaux, near Paris. The wedding was followed by a somewhat unusual honeymoon—the Curies set off on their bicycles around the French countryside!

Monsieur and Madame Curie

Married life was a new challenge for Marie. Everything she did, she did to the best of her ability, and this was true of her marriage as well as her work. The eight or more hours of scientific research into the magnetism of steel, which she and Pierre carried out each day, were the easy part for Marie. What she found difficult was managing her household, even though it was only a tiny three-room apartment. Marie wanted to prepare wholesome meals for Pierre, but cooking came much harder to her than physics. Her recipe books have little notes in the margins—she kept track of her mistakes so she could avoid repeating them later!

Pierre and Marie bought their bicycles with some money given to them as a wedding present by a cousin. They used them for vacations for years to come.

The Great Work Begins

In 1897, Marie Curie was expecting her first child and working on the publication of her first major research into magnetism. Her pregnancy made her ill and tired, but she refused to rest, instead setting off on the usual summer bicycle trip with Pierre. Marie was very disappointed when she had to give up and go back to Paris, but on September 12, she gave birth to a healthy daughter, Irène.

A juggling act

Marie was determined that she would continue with her scientific work, as well as look after her daughter. However, she found leaving Irène with a nurse very hard, and would often rush from the laboratory just to check that the child was safe.

Life was made much easier by Pierre's father. Pierre's mother died of breast **cancer** shortly after baby Irène was born, and Pierre's father moved in with his son and daughter-in-law. Knowing that her precious daughter was being watched over and taught by her devoted grandfather made it much easier for Marie to focus on her work.

*While Marie Curie was busy trying to combine research with family life, Antoine-Henri Becquerel was making important discoveries about **radiation**.*

The humidity and temperature in Marie's workroom changed all the time, making careful scientific measurements almost impossible. It was all that was available, however, and Marie set out to make the best of it.

A doctor's thesis

At the end of 1897, Marie set her next target—she wanted to earn a **doctorate.** Her imagination was caught by the findings of Becquerel. His work on the rays produced by **uranium** was so new that the field for research was wide open, and thus ideal for working on for a doctor's thesis. Where did the energy come from and what was it made of? These were the questions that drove Marie on, and she was given the use of a glassed-in, damp, and crowded storeroom at the bottom of the School of Physics to begin her work.

ANTOINE-HENRI BECQUEREL

In February 1896, Antoine-Henri Becquerel (1852–1908) was the first person to observe the natural **radioactivity** of uranium and to propose the presence of previously unknown rays. Becquerel's initial theory was that **X-rays** might be produced by **fluorescent** material. He was working with a uranium compound that fluoresces when it is exposed to sunlight. As luck would have it, the sun did not shine for several days, and Becquerel left his uranium sample and a photographic plate in a drawer. Eventually, when the cloudy weather showed no signs of lifting, he decided to develop the plate anyway. It was heavily fogged—showing that radiation had been emitted by the uranium compound without the stimulation of sunlight.

Radioactivity!

Shut away in her damp and gloomy storeroom, Marie Curie worked furiously. Her apparatus was not complex—she had an **ionization chamber** to show up **radiation,** a Curie **electrometer,** and a **piezoelectric quartz**—but she struggled to keep everything working accurately in the poor conditions of her makeshift "laboratory." In spite of all the difficulties, however, interesting results soon began to emerge.

Radioactivity emerges

First, Marie showed that the intensity of the radiation produced by **uranium** depended only on the amount of uranium present. The relationship between the amount of uranium and the amount of radiation was constant, and was not affected by light, temperature, or the chemical state of the uranium. These results were of vital importance in showing that the radiation discovered by Becquerel really was a new and unique phenomenon, probably a property of the very uranium **atoms** themselves.

Then Marie moved on—was uranium the only **element** to possess this new property, or did other elements produce these

This page from Marie Curie's workbook was written on February 6, 1898, and shows her neat columns of figures as she recorded her results. She noted that the temperature was 6.25 °C (43.25 °F), followed by ten exclamation marks to show her disapproval of such chilly working conditions!

Marie studied tirelessly to discover more about radioactivity.

strange rays as well? In a rush of enthusiasm, she started to examine all the known chemical elements of the time. The result she hoped for was not long in coming—compounds of the element thorium also emitted rays like those of uranium. This showed that the phenomenon was not unique to uranium, and needed its own name. Marie Curie suggested **"radioactivity."**

Not content with this discovery, Marie then began to examine different **ores** and **minerals.** As she expected, only the ores containing uranium and thorium showed radioactivity.

However, when she studied these minerals in detail, her results showed more radiation being given off than should have resulted from the amount of uranium or thorium present. Her first assumption was that her results were wrong, and with painstaking care she redid them all twenty times, but the results were consistently the same. Marie had already tested all the known elements for radioactivity. This new source of radioactivity, far more powerful than uranium or thorium, could mean only one thing—she had discovered a new element!

In Curie's words:

Marie and Pierre went over and over the evidence and were convinced. As Marie said to her sister Bronya: *"The radiation I couldn't explain comes from a new chemical element. The element is there and I've got to find it. We are sure!…I am convinced I am not mistaken!"*

The New Elements

Marie's early discoveries were so exciting that Pierre decided to leave his research on crystals and join his wife in her search for the new **element.** Two great scientific brains focused on the task made the work progress much faster. The couple shared observations, wrote joint papers and shared the credit for the work they performed.

Pitchblende was the uranium ore from which the Curies discovered two new elements.

The secret of pitchblende

Marie and Pierre concentrated their work on the **uranium ore** called **pitchblende.** Bit by bit, they separated it into the various elements of which it was made, and then looked for **radioactivity** in each of these elements. To their astonishment, after eliminating the uranium, they still had two sources of radioactivity. They had discovered not one, but two new elements! Marie named the first **polonium** after Poland, her beloved birthplace. The second they named **radium.** It was the more stable, radioactive, and useful of the two.

In the Curies' words:

The papers Marie and Pierre wrote at the time show how completely their work was intertwined. Although they each kept an individual laboratory notebook where they recorded the details of their experiments, they always wrote *"We found…"* or *"We observed…"* in their published papers, avoiding having to identify who actually did what: *"Certain **minerals**…are very active from the point of view of the emission of Becquerel rays. In a preceding communication, one of us showed that their activity was even greater than that of uranium or thorium."* Was it Marie or Pierre? It was their intention that no one should know.

A busy year

In 1898, the year that Marie discovered two new radioactive elements, she was also busy in her personal life. Notes in her diaries and letters reveal her making gooseberry jam and recording baby Irène's first steps and words.

The final proof

Some of the Curies' fellow scientists at the university did not share their belief in the new elements. To convince them that radium and polonium existed, the Curies needed to isolate the pure elements, yet they could not afford to buy the amount of ore they needed to do this.

Marie realized that waste from the glass industry—left after uranium salts had been extracted from pitchblende—would be cheap to buy, but would still contain radium and polonium. She arranged for tons of the industrial waste to be brought from Bohemia. It took nearly four years (1898–1902) of hard labor in harsh conditions to melt and treat the pitchblende waste and to extract the tiny amounts of radioactive materials within.

They were utterly absorbed in their work and, at home, in their daughter. It was a time of great fulfillment and happiness for Marie Curie. Finally, in 1902, she had prepared one-tenth of a gram of pure radium, and determined its **atomic weight** as 226. Any doubting fellow scientists were silenced for good— radium officially existed as a newly-discovered element.

*Marie Curie used this **ionization chamber** in her search to discover the source of radioactivity.*

A Gift of Healing

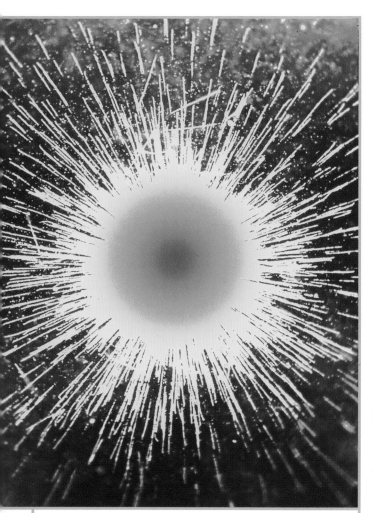

*What is radium? It is an **element** that:*
- *gives off radiation over a million times more intense than that of **uranium***
- *gives off a gaseous substance which was known as "radium emanation"—now called radon*
- *gives off heat as it decays*
- *makes an impression on photographic plates*
- *makes the atmosphere a conductor of electricity.*

Radium salts are luminous (they give off light).

Radium had been the focus of the Curies' life for several years before they isolated it. During this time, they also had to work as teachers at the university, to earn enough money to live on. After Pierre's modesty caused him to be passed over for several prestigious positions—in spite of his great talent—Marie took on a teaching post at a girls' school to earn extra money. Bowed down by too much work, too little food, and too much radiation, the health of the Curies began to suffer.

Family problems

Several tragedies struck the little family. Marie's beloved father died; she gave birth prematurely to a little girl, who died; and then her nephew, Bronya's son, died of the disease meningitis. On top of this, Pierre was suffering from severe pains in his legs. Yet in spite of all these setbacks, the Curies kept working on their beloved radium.

Radium and cancer

The Curies discovered that radium "burned" the skin, destroying the tissue. As an experiment, Pierre burned his arm and watched as the skin slowly healed. They quickly recognized that radium might be used to destroy cancerous growths. **Radium therapy**—and the radium industry—was born.

Ernest Rutherford (left) and Frederick Soddy (right) were making many discoveries about the nature of **radioactivity** at the time when Marie Curie was doing her work on radium. Rutherford named the three types of rays—**alpha, beta,** and **gamma radiation**—while together they developed the atomic disintegration theory of radioactivity. This explains that the **nucleus** of a radioactive substance splits to form other elements, releasing energy in the form of radiation.

In 1903, Marie became the first woman in France to earn a **doctorate.** Shortly afterward, she and Pierre made an important decision. They had developed the technique for the isolation of radium from spent **pitchblende,** and now there was a huge medical market for the rare **element.** People all over the world were asking for details on how to extract radium.

The Curies had a choice: they could publish their results freely for anyone to use, or they could **patent** their methods, which would limit their use and also make the Curies very wealthy. For Marie, though, there was no choice—patenting would be against the scientific spirit. In making this decision, the Curies made radium treatment available to thousands, but condemned themselves to many more years of poverty and difficult work without a proper laboratory.

Tragedy Strikes

Finally, after years of solitary toil, Marie and Pierre began to be rewarded as their work was recognized by fellow scientists. But although they did not know it, they were moving toward the end of their immensely creative working partnership.

France gave Marie and Pierre Curie very little support or recognition, but other countries were more perceptive. In 1903, the **Royal Society of London** awarded the **Davy Medal** to the Curies.

Later that same year, it was announced that the **Nobel prize** for physics was to be split between Antoine-Henri Becquerel and Marie and Pierre Curie for their work on **radioactivity.** This meant not just recognition, but also a very large sum of money, so Pierre could do less teaching, and they could save for a proper laboratory. The money was very welcome, but the attentions of the press and other well-wishers were not!

Only after the award of the Nobel prize did the Sorbonne offer Pierre Curie a professorship of physics. He was happy to accept the job, but bitter that in France, recognition of their work had taken so long to come.

A beginning and an ending

In 1904, Marie and Pierre were delighted by the birth of their second daughter, Eve. Although the children were cared for by servants, allowing both parents to continue their work, time in the evenings and on holidays was set aside to spend together, and the little family was close and affectionate. Marie and Pierre relished their shared work and their home life. Their marriage was truly a joining of two great minds; they were almost constant companions, and they loved each other deeply.

April 19, 1906 was a wet, gloomy day. Pierre walked along the crowded, busy streets of Paris to the laboratory, absorbed as usual in his thoughts. He stepped out from behind a cab to cross the road—and walked straight into the path of a large wagon, drawn by a team of horses. The driver could not stop the wagon, and the left back wheel totally crushed Pierre's skull. In an instant, Pierre Curie was dead.

The devastation and grief that the death of her beloved husband brought to Marie Curie can never be measured. In one brief moment, she had lost her partner in life and in work, the father of her children, and her closest friend. She never fully recovered from the loss.

When Pierre Curie was killed at the age of 46, the world lost one of its greatest scientific minds.

In Curie's words:

Marie recorded in her diary some of her thoughts as she sat with the body of her husband: *"Pierre, my Pierre, you are there, calm as a poor wounded man resting in sleep, with his head bandaged. Your face is sweet and serene, it is still you, lost in a dream from which you cannot get out."*

The Work Goes On

Marie Curie drove herself as hard as possible to do her work and bring up her two daughters, while continuing to grieve deeply for her lost partner.

In Curie's words:

Marie's diary entries after Pierre's death show her turmoil and distress:

May 11, 1906: "My Pierre, I got up after having slept rather well, relatively calm. That was only a quarter of an hour ago, and now I want to howl again—like a wild beast."

June 10, 1906: "Everything is gloomy..."

For several months, Marie was devastated. She dressed in black, and was utterly absorbed in her loss, unable even to take comfort in her daughters. Then she was offered the chance to take over Pierre's professorship and to direct research at the School of Physics. It was the first time such a post had ever been offered to a woman. Full of uncertainty, she accepted.

Filling Pierre's shoes

On Monday, November 5, 1906, at 1:30 P.M., Marie Curie became the first woman to deliver a lecture in the Sorbonne, the great University of Paris. She began her lecture at the precise sentence where Pierre had left off all those months before, and spoke with authority on new theories in **physics.** Thus she took up the challenge of her new life alone, supporting her family and continuing her work. Pierre's father still lived with them, helping Marie with the two little girls as she struggled to balance her work with raising her children.

Back to work

Marie continued working with **radium** and **polonium.** She once again measured the **atomic weight** of radium and separated the pure metal for the first and only time. Radium is almost always found and used combined with other **elements** in radium salts. In order to prove that it was an element, and to ensure its chemical character could be fully understood, Marie undertook this very precise work. As **radium therapy** for **cancer** treatment continued to be developed, she also worked out a way of measuring minute amounts of radium by the **radiation** they produce, so that the correct doses for treatment could be calculated.

The second Nobel prize

Marie again had trouble finding recognition for her work in France when the Academy of Sciences refused her entry as a member in 1911. But in December of that same year, the Swedish Academy of Sciences, recognizing the brilliant work Marie had done since Pierre's death, awarded her the **Nobel prize** in chemistry. To win one Nobel prize is the ultimate acknowledgement; to win two is unbelievable—yet Marie Curie, with her humble Polish background and constant lack of money, had done it.

In July 1914, three years after Marie was awarded her second Nobel prize, the Radium Institute was opened in Paris. It was known as the Curie Pavilion and was built on Rue Pierre Curie (Pierre Curie Street). At last, Marie had the laboratory that she and Pierre had dreamed of—it was just too late for them to share it.

Not long after Marie Curie was awarded her second **Nobel prize,** her health failed her badly. She had to have surgery on her kidneys, and it took her a long time to recover. She recuperated, spending time with her daughters and a group of friends that included Albert Einstein—who had become world-famous when he developed his **theory of relativity**—and his son. Einstein and Marie Curie spent hours discussing ideas, some of which formed the beginning of Einstein's groundbreaking work.

By 1914, Marie's life was more stable. The girls were growing up—Irène was 17 and Eve was 10—the Curie Pavilion had been opened, her research was going well, and she had rented a vacation house in northern France for the summers. But a new cloud was building on the horizon—the conflict that turned into World War I.

The outbreak of war

When the war started, Marie realized that **X-rays,** which she had studied closely, could be useful in helping to treat wounded soldiers, since they were an excellent tool for finding foreign objects, such as bullets and pieces of **shrapnel** lodged in the body. First, she borrowed all available X-ray machines from laboratories and moved them to hospitals, but soon realized that the equipment was really needed out in the field.

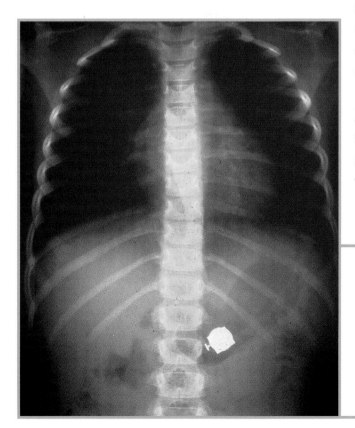

X-rays are of enormous value in identifying broken bones, and they also reveal any foreign body, such as a bullet or an object that has been swallowed by accident. The person in this X-ray has swallowed a wristwatch.

This is Marie Curie in 1914, at the wheel of the Renault that she converted into her first "radiological car."

The "radiological car"

It did not take Marie long to solve the problem of getting X-ray equipment out to the troops where it was needed. She took an ordinary car and fitted it with a Roentgen apparatus and a **dynamo,** which could be driven by the engine of the car, to power the X-ray machine.

As the war progressed into a long and bloody conflict, Marie organized the manufacture and equipping of twenty of these radiological cars, which were then sent to the front line. Known as "little Curies," they carried the X-ray equipment to the field hospitals full of injured and dying men.

Marie also set up 200 radiological rooms at military hospitals, making it possible for over a million wounded men to be examined. She drove herself relentlessly, as always, returning home only when she was ill herself.

WILHELM ROENTGEN

In 1895, Wilhelm Konrad Roentgen (1845–1923) was investigating materials that **fluoresce** when they are exposed to **cathode rays.** In doing his work, he discovered new rays that also caused fluorescence, but penetrated the paper and metal that stopped the cathode rays. Roentgen had discovered X-rays. Within days of his announcement, doctors began to use them to see inside the human body without cutting it open.

The American Connection

Winning two **Nobel prizes** had given Marie Curie enough money to live and work without concern. But during the war, she contributed all of her money to the French war effort, and lost it all. When peace was restored, funding for research became a problem once more. However, this time help came from an unexpected direction.

An American benefactor

Mrs. William Brown Meloney was editor of an important New York magazine and well-known in American society. For years, she had wanted to meet Marie Curie, and eventually a brief interview was organized. What Mrs. Meloney discovered, to her amazement, was that Marie Curie's new laboratory had little or no equipment and only one gram of **radium,** which was used solely for the treatment of **cancer.** The United States, on the other hand, had about 50 grams of radium. Marie Curie needed a gram of radium to continue her research, but she could not afford the $100,000 needed to buy it.

In Mrs. Meloney's words:

Mrs. Meloney was completely overawed when she finally met Marie Curie. In an account she wrote afterward, she said: *"My timidity exceeded her own. I had been a trained interrogator for twenty years, but I could not ask a single question of this gentle woman…I tried to explain that American women were interested in her great work and found myself apologizing for intruding on her precious time…"*

Mrs. William Brown Meloney was an American woman who raised funds for Marie Curie.

A visit to the United States

Mrs. Meloney went home inspired and determined that she and the women of the United States would do something to help. She launched the Marie Curie Radium Fund in her home country, appealing especially to women, and in less than a year the money had been raised. She invited Marie to come to the United States with her daughters to receive her radium. It was a measure of Marie's gratitude that at the age of 53, she undertook the longest journey of her life.

In the U.S., Marie was constantly surrounded by people. She appreciated the concern and support of her new friends, but found it almost more than her fragile health could bear. At the end of the visit, Marie was exhausted, but content. She felt that she had contributed to the friendship between the United States, France, and Poland; she had won many hearts and gained a lifelong friend in Mrs. Meloney—and she also had her precious gram of radium.

In 1921, Marie Curie received a gram of radium from the president of the United States himself, Warren G. Harding, at a special ceremony.

Death by Radium

After the successful trip to America, Marie continued her work with **radium.** Since the end of the war, she had been aided by her daughter Irène; in 1924, Frédéric Joliot, who would become Irène's husband, joined them. The three of them took great pleasure in working together, sharing ideas along with family life.

Failing health

As a young student, Marie Curie had eaten poorly and made herself ill. Once she started working on **radioactivity,** she took no precautions, handling her beloved radium with bare hands and unshaded eyes. Even when it had become apparent that the **element** caused burns, and other workers were beginning to protect themselves by using gloves and goggles, Marie refused to let anything come between her and the element she and her husband had discovered. As she got older, she began to pay the price for her pioneering work.

In 1923, she was threatened with blindness when **cataracts** took her sight, but surgery restored her vision. The damage to her internal organs, however, could not be repaired so easily.

Marie and her daughter Irène took great pleasure in working together, just as Marie and Pierre had done.

The face of Marie Curie in old age reflects the hard work and sadness that filled much of her life. She gave a great deal to the world, and took very little.

Last days

In 1934, Marie left her beloved laboratory for the last time, feeling dreadfully ill. Her health went into an irreversible downward spiral. She was increasingly weak and tired, with high fevers and pain, but doctors could not decide what was wrong with her. She was sent to a nursing home in the mountains, where her devoted younger daughter Eve took care of her as she grew weaker and weaker. Finally, at dawn on July 4, 1934, Marie Curie gave up the battle for life. The doctor who had cared for her reported that she died of "aplastic pernicious **anemia** of rapid, feverish development. The bone marrow did not react, probably because it had been injured by a long accumulation of **radiations.**" Marie's precious radium was the cause of her death. At the relatively young age of 66, she was buried with her beloved Pierre, in the family tomb at Sceaux. Her life's work was over.

IRÈNE AND FRÉDÉRIC JOLIOT-CURIE

Irène and Frédéric Joliot-Curie formed another close-knit husband and wife team. Working in the Radium Institute, the Joliot-Curies were the first to develop an artificial radioactive element—a radioactive form of phosphorus. This work won them the **Nobel prize** for chemistry in 1935. In 1939, they demonstrated that the fission (splitting) of **uranium** can lead to a **chain reaction,** a discovery that has had a major effect both on the development of nuclear weapons and of nuclear power.

A Force for Good

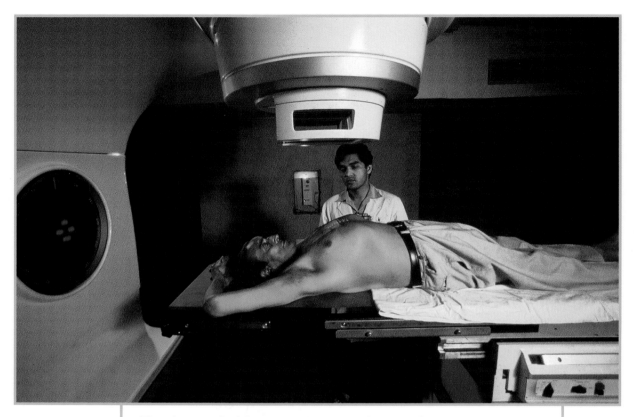

The therapy first begun in the time of Marie Curie is still saving lives today, in a more sophisticated form.

The **radium** that Marie and Pierre Curie isolated with such painstaking care, and the work that Marie continued to do on her own into the nature of **radioactivity,** left a long-term legacy from which we still benefit today.

The **cancer** treatment they developed will continue to save lives well into the 21st century. "Curietherapy" has been refined and developed a great deal, but radiotherapy using radium is still very important in the treatment of cancers. Methods of delivering the radioactivity to exactly the right place are improving all the time. Other radioactive materials can be used to trace pathways in the body and to help doctors treat a wide variety of conditions without having to resort to surgery.

The pioneering work of Marie Curie has also led to a wide range of applications beyond the field of medicine, where radium and other radioactive **elements** are so widely used.

Food preservation

For centuries, the main methods of preserving food remained the same: salting, drying, cooling, and pickling. More recently, freezing and canning were developed. Late in the twentieth century, another new method of food preservation was discovered, called irradiation. If food is exposed to a low dose of **radiation,** the bacteria and mold on it are killed very effectively, considerably prolonging the life of the products. This is a big advantage to the people selling the food, but there has been some resistance from consumers who feel they are getting little benefit and perhaps some increased risk.

Electricity without strings?

Irène and Frédéric Joliot-Curie carried on the work they started with Marie Curie, eventually showing that when **uranium** decays, it can set up a **chain reaction.** If the energy produced in that chain reaction is controlled, it can be used to drive turbines and make electricity in a nuclear power station.

Electricity can be generated in a nuclear power station using a controlled chain reaction.

As the 21st century begins, people all over the world are becoming increasingly dependent on electricity. Yet most of the traditional methods of producing electricity depend on burning fossil fuels such as oil and coal. This raises two large problems—it creates a lot of pollution, and fossil fuels are being rapidly depleted. In an ideal world, nuclear power would be the clean and pollution-free way to make electricity. It has not yet worked out like this, however, because radioactive waste causes problems of its own. But as reserves of fossil fuels get used up, nuclear power may become more important in the future.

The Dark Side

This "mushroom cloud" formed over Nagasaki, Japan after the dropping of an atomic bomb in 1945. When the bombs were dropped, no one knew for sure how much energy would be released, or what the effects would be on the surrounding area. Only when the "mushroom clouds" had died away and the war was over were the effects of these experimental bombs able to be measured.

Marie Curie recognized that, while the work she was doing held great potential for good, there was also the possibility that the power she had discovered could be used for evil purposes.

The work started by Marie, and continued by her daughter Irène and her husband, led to a rapidly growing understanding of **radioactivity** and what happens in a **chain reaction.** During World War II, fears grew that Nazi Germany would use this knowledge to develop a nuclear weapon. This resulted in the setting up of the Manhattan Project in the U.S. to develop a nuclear weapon first. Although the war with Germany ended in May 1945, the war with Japan continued. In August 1945, the only atomic bombs ever to be used in warfare were dropped on the Japanese cities of Hiroshima and Nagasaki. The Japanese surrendered on September 2, 1945, and World War II was over.

Brighter than a thousand suns

The atomic explosions were devastating. The light burned the eyeballs and blinded many of those who saw it. People were literally **vaporized.** Thousands more died in the following days from severe burns and **radiation** sickness. For years to come, more people died from the type of **anemia** that had killed Marie Curie herself, and from **cancers** triggered by the massive radiation doses they had received. Babies were born with severe birth defects, caused by the effects of radiation, and many other children developed cancers that were linked to the radiation their parents had been exposed to. Scientists are still collecting evidence on the long-term effects of the dropping of those two nuclear bombs.

A shadow over the future

During the **Cold War** between the former Soviet Union and the West in the 1960s, 70s, and 80s, fears of war and of the sabotage of nuclear power stations were high. This led to billions of dollars being spent on stockpiles of nuclear weapons, with the capacity to destroy the whole planet many times over. Although the threat of nuclear war has largely been lifted with the breakup of the former Soviet Union in 1991, fear of nuclear weapons in the wrong hands is one legacy from the work of Marie Curie that is unlikely ever to leave us.

This U.S. nuclear missile, the Titan II, was built in 1963, at the height of the Cold War. It was capable of flying over 5,000 miles (8,000 kilometers)—far enough to cross the Atlantic.

A Woman who Stands Alone

Even though the Curie family was spread through Poland, Austria, and France, the bond between Marie (left) and her brother and sisters was strong, and they remained closely involved in each other's lives.

Marie Curie traveled a very long way in her lifetime. From her beginnings in Russian-controlled Poland, she became one of the greatest scientists of her time. Her discoveries rank with the greatest, and her work is still of enormous importance.

Marie's early childhood was happy, if hard. She had loving parents, and sisters and a brother with whom she played and enjoyed all the pleasures of family life. Although they had their share of tragedies, with the loss of both their oldest sister and their mother, the family was close-knit and supportive of each other throughout their lives.

A finely focused mind

Once Marie moved to Paris and began her studies, she showed the most remarkable focus on her work. Her determination to study and shine in the sciences led her to ignore almost everything else. Her dedication was rewarded, however, not only in the amazing discoveries she made, but also in the deep love she shared with her husband, Pierre Curie.

Their incredible discovery of two new radioactive **elements** was all the more astonishing because of the dreadful conditions in which they had to work. It was the supreme tragedy of Marie's life that Pierre was killed while they were still relatively young. Although she continued her work, which could hardly have been more impressive if Pierre had lived, she carried at all times a deep sadness over his loss.

A scientist of genius

The stature of Marie's work on **radioactivity** can be measured in the fact that she was awarded not one, but two **Nobel prizes**—and this at a time when women were rarely encouraged—or allowed—to go beyond their traditional roles as housewives and mothers. Marie proved that it was possible to combine motherhood with a brilliant career. She fulfilled all of her academic promise and died while still engaged in her work, her body destroyed by the **radiation** to which she had devoted so much of her life. She was one of the greatest scientists of all time.

The legacy of Marie Curie lives on in medicine, in power generation and industry, and in weapons of war. She was a woman of genius.

Timeline

1859	Pierre Curie is born on May 15 in France.
1867	Marya Sklodovska (later Marie Curie) is born on November 7 in Warsaw, in Russian-occupied Poland.
1873	Marie's father loses his savings after poor investments.
1878	Her mother dies of **tuberculosis.**
1879	The scientist Albert Einstein is born in Germany.
1883	Marie leaves secondary school with honors—she is awarded the gold medal for best pupil.
1884	Marie and Bronya become involved in the "Floating University."
1885	Marie starts work as a **governess.** Bronya begins medical studies in Paris.
1888	Marie leaves her job as a governess.
1890	Bronya marries Casimir Dluski.
1891	Marie goes to Paris to study science.
1894	Meets Pierre Curie.
1895	Marries Pierre Curie on July 26. Wilhelm Roentgen discovers **X-rays.**
1896	Antoine-Henri Becquerel demonstrates that **uranium** salts emit rays of an unknown nature without exposure to light.
1897	Marie and Pierre's first daughter, Irène, is born. Marie starts work on her **doctorate.**
1898	Marie discovers two new **radioactive elements—polonium** and **radium.**
1900	Pierre becomes a lecturer at the Sorbonne.
1903	Marie becomes the first woman in France to earn a doctorate. Marie and Pierre are awarded the **Davy Medal** by the **Royal Society of London,** and share the **Nobel prize** for physics with Antoine-Henri Becquerel.
1904	Marie and Pierre's second daughter, Eve, is born. Pierre is appointed professor at the Sorbonne.
1906	On April 19, Pierre Curie is killed in a traffic accident in Paris. On November 5, Marie becomes the first woman to deliver a lecture at the Sorbonne, the University of Paris.

1911	Marie is awarded the **Nobel prize** for chemistry.
1914	The Radium Institute—the Curie Pavilion—opens in Paris.
1914–18	World War I. Marie organizes "radiological cars" to examine soldiers by X-ray in the field.
1918	Marie's daughter Irène starts to work in her mother's lab.
1921	Marie travels to the United States to receive a gram of radium purchased with $100,000 raised by the Marie Curie Radium Fund.
1924	Frédéric Joliot starts to work with Marie and Irène.
1926	Irène marries Frédéric Joliot.
1934	On July 4, Marie Curie dies of **cancer** caused by **radiation.**
1935	Irène and Frédéric Joliot-Curie win the Nobel prize for chemistry for producing the first artificial radioactive substances.
1945	Two atomic bombs dropped on the Japanese cities of Hiroshima and Nagasaki.

More Books to Read

Birch, Beverley. *Marie Curie's Search for Radium.* Hauppage, N.Y.: Barron's Educational Series, Inc., 1995.

Burby, Liza N. *Marie Curie.* New York: Rosen Publishing Group, Inc., 1997.

Parker, Steve. *Marie Curie & Radium.* Broomall, Penn.: Chelsea House Publishers, 1995.

Glossary

alpha ray radiation consisting of alpha particles, or helium nuclei

anemia shortage of red blood cells

annex to take over by force

atom smallest particle of an element that still has all its properties

atomic weight combined value of the protons and the neutrons in the nucleus of an atom; now known as the atomic mass or nucleon number

banishment being required by the authorities to leave a country

beta ray radiation consisting of streams of beta particles or electrons

cancer uncontrolled growth of cells to form a tumor

cataract clouding of the lens of the eye that can impair vision

cathode ray flow of high energy electrons

chain reaction self-sustaining nuclear reaction in which the neutrons produced by the splitting of one atom cause the splitting of more atoms, and the neutrons from this cause further splittings, and so on

Cold War time of unfriendly relations (but no actual warfare) between the United States and communist countries

Davy Medal one of the highest awards given by the Royal Society, in memory of the scientist Sir Humphry Davy

dignitary important person

doctorate high-level degree, such as a Doctor of Philosophy (Ph.D.) or a Doctor of Science

dynamo machine for converting mechanical energy into electrical energy

electrometer apparatus for measuring voltage

element substance made up of only one type of atom

fluoresce to give off visible light in response to exposure to external radiation, such as sunlight

gamma ray strong, penetrating type of radiation

governess someone who teaches the children of a family at their own home, often living with the family as well

ionization chamber special chamber which allows ionizing radiation to be detected and analyzed

master's degree degree earned after a first degree, usually on completion of research or graduate school studies

mineral substance found in rock

Nobel prize award given by the Nobel Foundation for outstanding achievement in physics, chemistry, medicine, literature, economics, or for the promotion of world peace

nucleus central part of an atom containing protons and neutrons. The nucleus of an atom contains virtually all of its mass.

ore rock containing a compound of a metal—the metal can be extracted from the ore

patent permission granted by a government to allow an inventor to make, use, and sell an invention for a set period of time. Anyone else wishing to use that procedure or invention has to pay the original inventor.

pension money paid to someone to support them during retirement

periodic table way of arranging the chemical elements according to the numbers of electrons in their atoms

physics study of matter, energy, and their interactions

piezoelectric quartz crystal that distorts when a voltage is applied to it

pitchblende uranium-containing ore

polonium first radioactive element discovered by Marie Curie; named after Poland

radiation particles or rays given off by radioactive nuclei

radioactivity emission of radiation by a nucleus as it decays

radium radioactive element discovered by Marie Curie

radium therapy treatment for cancer using the radiation from radium to destroy cancer cells

Royal Society of London very prestigious academic society

scholarship money granted to a student to cover educational costs

shrapnel fragments of an exploded bomb, mine, or shell

theory of relativity idea that all motion can only be measured relative to something else—therefore, nothing is absolute

tuberculosis bacterial disease, widespread in the nineteenth and early twentieth centuries, that affects many parts of the body, but particularly the lungs; often known as TB

typhus infectious fever characterized by a purple rash, headaches, and fever

uranium radioactive element

vaporized turned into a vapor, or gas

voltage measure of electric force

X-ray ray of very short wavelength that can penetrate matter too dense for light rays to pass through, such as skin

Index